G000269041

WEATHER AND SEASONS

WEATHER AND SEASONS

through the eyes of artists

Dry September © Monica Poole

Wendy and Jack Richardson

First published by Heinemann Library, 1993, a division of Heinemann Publishers (Oxford) Ltd, Halley Court, Jordan Hill, Oxford OX2 8EJ.

OXFORD LONDON EDINBURGH
MADRID PARIS ATHENS BOLOGNA
MELBOURNE SYDNEY AUCKLAND SINGAPORE TOKYO
IBADAN NAIROBI GABORONE HARARE
PORTSMOUTH NH (USA)

98 97 96 95 94
10 9 8 7 6 5 4 3 2

Series editing by Zoë Books Ltd
Picture research by Faith Perkins
Design by Mike Brain

Printed in China

British Library Cataloguing in Publication Data
is available from the British Library on request.

ISBN 0-431-00981-3

Photographic acknowledgements
The authors and publishers wish to acknowledge with thanks the following photographic sources:
Cover and p33: Four Trees – Egon Schiele. Österreichische Galerie, Vienna. Fotostudio Otto
Title Page: Dry September – © Monica Poole
Frontispiece: Gabriele Münter, aged 28 (photo by Kandinsky) – © Gabriele Münter and Johannes Eichner – Stiftung.
Botticelli – Galleria degli Uffizi, Florence. Scala p6
La Primavera – Galleria degli Uffizi, Florence. Scala pp6–7
Spring Bank. 1974 – Collection: Centre Nationale d'Art et Culture © Helen Frankenthaler 1991. Photographie Musée National d'Art Moderne, Centre Georges Pompidou, Paris. Jacqueline Hyde pp8–9
Palmer by G. Richmond – By courtesy of the National Portrait Gallery, London p10
In a Shoreham Garden – By courtesy of the Board of Trustees of the Victoria and Albert Museum, London p11
Seurat by Maximilien Luce – Bibliothèque Nationale, Paris p12
The Seine at La Grande Jatte in the Spring – Musées Royaux des Beaux-Arts de Belgique, Brussels (photo: G. Cussac) pp12–13
Spring Hoeing – Sally and Richard Greenhill pp14–5
Turner – Self portrait, aged 15. By courtesy of the National Portrait Gallery, London p16
Landscape with Distant River and Bay – Musée du Louvre, Paris. © photograph RMN pp16–17
Brueghel the Elder – The Mansell Collection p18
The Harvesters – The Metropolitan Museum of Art, New York. Rogers Fund, 1919 pp18–19
Bonnard – Self-portrait. Private Collection, New York © ADAGP/SPADEM, Paris and DACS, London 1993. Giraudon p20
The Palm – Bonnard. The Phillips Collection, Washington, D.C. © ADAGP/SPADEM, Paris and DACS, London 1993 pp20–1
Münter – © Gabriele Münter – und Johannes Eichner – Stiftung p22
Jawlensky and Werefkin in a Field – © Gabriele Münter – und Johannes Eichner – Stiftung. Städtische Galerie im Lenbachhaus, Munich pp22–3
Millais by W. Holman Hunt – By courtesy of the National Portrait Gallery, London p24
Autumn Leaves – Manchester City Art Galleries p25
Kandinsky – Bildarchiv Preussischer Kulturbesitz, Berlin p26
Painting Number 199. 1914 – The Museum of Modern Art, New York. Nelson A. Rockefeller Fund (by exchange). © ADAGP, Paris and DACS, London 1993 p27
Goya – Museo del Prado, Madrid. © photo ARXIU MAS p28
The Wine Harvest (Autumn) – Museo del Prado, Madrid. © photo ARXIU MAS p29
Corot – Musée du Louvre, Paris. Giraudon p30
The Gust of Wind – Musée du Louvre, Paris. Lauros-Giraudon pp30–1
Schiele – Bild-Archiv der Österreichischen Nationalbibliothek, Vienna. Photo Lichtbildwerkstätte "Alpenland" p32
Four Trees – Österreichische Galerie, Vienna pp32–3
Hockney – Camera Press p34
A Man Stood In Front of his House with Rain Descending – © David Hockney. Museum van Hedendaagse Kunst, Belgium p35
Landscape at Pentecost (Turamurra) – Art Gallery of South Australia, Adelaide. South Australian Government Grant 1981 pp36–7
Ōi, from the Sixty-nine Stations on the Kisokaido – By courtesy of the Board of Trustees of the Victoria and Albert Museum, London pp38–9
Monet – Musée du Louvre, Paris. Giraudon p40
The Magpie – Musée d'Orsay, Paris. © photograph RMN pp40–1
Winter Landscape – Musée du Louvre, Paris. © photograph RMN pp42–3
Grandma Moses at her Painting Table – © 1987 Grandma Moses Properties Co., New York. Photo by Ifor Thomas p44
Hoosick Falls in Winter – The Phillips Collection, Washington. © 1987 Grandma Moses Properties Co., New York pp44–5

Portraits are by the artists themselves, unless stated otherwise.

The publishers have made every effort to trace the copyright holders, but if they have inadvertently overlooked any, they will be pleased to make the necessary arrangement at the first opportunity.

Contents

Gabriele Münter, aged 28 (photo by Kandinsky)

Introduction

This is a book of pictures about the weather and the seasons of the year. All over the world, people depend upon the changing seasons, so it is no surprise that many artists, from many places, have chosen to make pictures about them. Most of the pictures in the book are paintings, but two are prints. The pictures look very different, but they have one thing in common. They were made by people who thought that the best way to share their ideas was through pictures. So this is a book for you to look at.

The pictures tell how the artists felt about each of the seasons and the weather it brings. Some of the paintings are very serious. Others take a more light-hearted view. Some are about real events. Some are imaginary. Some show how things looked, some how they felt.

You will see how differently the idea of weather has made each of the artists feel, and you will have different feelings yourself as you look at each of the pictures. The weather and the seasons are something we have all experienced. Perhaps these pictures will help you to be more aware of the changing seasons.

For those who are interested in the weather

You may have chosen this book because you are interested in the weather and the seasons. Monet painted the changing seasons over and over again. They never ceased to fascinate him. If you begin to make pictures which show different seasons, you will see more clearly what is happening throughout the year.

For picture lovers

You may have chosen this book because you like looking at pictures. If so, perhaps you would like to see the original works. Many of the painters mentioned in the book spent time looking at the work of other artists and learning from it. A list at the beginning of the book tells you where to find those paintings which are on view to the public. They are in galleries all over the world, so you will not be able to see them all. Your nearest gallery may have other works by the artists you like.

For those who want to have a go themselves

You may have chosen this book because you like to draw or paint. If so, perhaps it will help you to discover some of the secrets of picture making. All the work in the book is the result of hard thinking, lots of practice and, above all, very careful looking. All the artists studied the world around them very closely. They noted what they saw, either in their minds or in notebooks. You could start a notebook now, as you watch the seasons change, and collect the information that will make your ideas come alive.

La Primavera

Tempera on wood 203 x 3.14 cm
Alessandro di Mariano Filipepi, known as Sandro Botticelli

Galleria degli Uffizi, Florence

LIVED:
c. 1445–1510

NATIONALITY:
Italian

TYPE OF WORK:
drawings and paintings

No one knows for sure what the subject of this painting is, but about 80 years after it was painted, Georgio Vasari, an artist and writer, called it *La Primavera*, which means 'Spring'. For many people it does seem to sum up the gentleness of spring when, as Shakespeare said, 'a young man's fancy lightly turns to thoughts of love'.

Painting myths and legends

When the picture was painted, educated people such as the wealthy Medici family who often asked Botticelli to paint pictures for them, were very interested in the myths and legends of Ancient Greece and Rome. They would certainly have known about the characters in the picture, and understood the story that Botticelli was telling.

The central figure is Venus, the goddess of love. A cupid, armed with arrows which he fires at people to make them fall in love, is flying above her. She gestures towards The Three Graces who dance together, clothed in pearls and fluttering silk. Flora, goddess of Spring and flowers, scatters rosebuds, while the earth nymph, Chloris, evades Zephyr, the west wind. Mercury, the messenger, dressed in sword and helmet, reaches upward with his snaky wand. Botticelli's graceful figures seem almost to float through the woodland.

A vision of female beauty

Botticelli was famous for his paintings of beautiful women. He shared his idea of beauty with many of the poets of the time. The faces of Venus, the Graces and the flower nymph are probably portraits of Simonetta Vespucci. Botticelli had painted Simonetta's portrait, and her delicate beauty matched his ideal. She died in Florence when she was only 23 years old.

Botticelli lived and worked very successfully in Florence. Then as he grew older, ill health, combined with the rising popularity of young painters such as Leonardo da Vinci and Michelangelo, meant that he lost many of his patrons and his fame. In the nineteenth century his pictures became popular again when they were rediscovered by a group of British painters known as the Pre-Raphaelite Brotherhood (see p. 24)

Galleria degli Uffizi, Florence

Spring Bank. 1974

Acrylic on canvas 269.2 x 274.3 cm
Helen Frankenthaler

BORN:
1928

NATIONALITY:
American

TYPE OF WORK:
paintings, sculptures, printmaking

Helen Frankenthaler was born into a wealthy New York family. At school, when she was 15 years old, she had a teacher who inspired in her a life-long passion for art. Her teacher was Rufino Tamayo, a Mexican painter who shared with Frankenthaler his love of bold colour and strong shapes. He also encouraged her to visit art galleries to study paintings of many kinds.

A life-long experiment with colour

When Frankenthaler was 17 years old she went to art college, where she was encouraged by her teachers to continue to experiment with colour. Over the years she developed a technique using very thin colour. First she stained the canvas without leaving brushmarks, so that the woven texture of the canvas showed through. She then painted thinly on this coloured canvas ground.

In the 1970s Frankenthaler began working in acrylic paint. She could thin this paint down until it was no longer solid colour, but allowed light to shine through it. It became translucent. Then she could overlap colours so that each area took on a new hue. Sometimes she gave an area of paint a hard edge, so that the colour change is sudden. Sometimes she blotted the edges so that one colour drifts into another.

Inspiration from the landscape

Frankenthaler's paintings are abstract, but the ideas for them often come from landscapes. For instance, this picture is called *Spring Bank*. What do you think the artist saw that made her want to paint the picture?

Green is the colour Frankenthaler has used most in this painting. It changes from soft blueish green to sharp acid green. Other colours range from the lightest tints to intense patches of purple and blue. A splash of orange, as fresh as the flesh of the fruit, is underlined by a band of cherry red. The colours glow like jewels. It is almost a relief to look at the pale, greyish colour washed over the warm brown.

Imagine how different the picture would be if you changed some of the colours around — perhaps the grey and the purple patches. What would be the effect on everything else?

Collection: Centre Nationale d'Art et Culture.

In a Shoreham Garden

Watercolour and body colour 27.9 x 22.2 cm
Samuel Palmer

By G. Richmond. By courtesy of the National Portrait Gallery, London

LIVED:
1805–1881

NATIONALITY:
British

TYPE OF WORK:
paintings and etchings

Blossom is the theme of this picture. The centre of the painting is one huge burst of blossom, thick on the tree like candy floss. Behind it is bright forsythia, the golden yellow bush which brightens spring gardens. Above the blossom, clouds scud across a showery sky. This is an English spring of the kind that Samuel Palmer knew well. For many years he lived in Shoreham, a village set in the orchards of Kent in southern England.

The picture has a slightly mysterious feeling. At the end of the path which leads us into the picture, Palmer has painted a woman. Though she is distant, she stands out clearly in a red dress. She gives the picture its mystery, and because she is so small, the garden seems huge.

Creating textures

Palmer was very interested in the textures he saw and felt. He worked in watercolour paint, which is usually spread thinly over wet paper, so that the light shines through it. Palmer has used watercolour in this way for the ground and the sky. He also used body paint, which is mixed with gum, to paint very thickly in blobs and trickles, making the rich surfaces he wanted.

The wonder of the world

Samuel Palmer was educated mainly at home. He was not a strong child, and he did not enjoy games or even playing outdoors. He preferred to be inside, reading, and as his father was a scholar and a bookseller there was always plenty to read. Palmer began to take an interest in drawing and when he was 13 years old he was given drawing lessons. He made very good progress. Only a year later three of his landscape drawings were exhibited at the Royal Academy in London. He was a very religious young man and he tried to show in his work not only what the world looked like, but his own great feeling of wonder for everything that God had made. It is this mystery and wonder that he has tried to show in his painting of the garden.

By courtesy of the Board of Trustees of the Victoria and Albert Museum. London

The Seine at La Grand Jatte in the Spring

Oil on canvas 65 x 81 cm
Georges Seurat

Bibliothèque Nationale, Paris

LIVED:
1859–1891

NATIONALITY:
French

TYPE OF WORK:
drawings and paintings

Georges Seurat developed a style of painting known as *Pointillism*. He had a scientist's attitude towards painting. First he studied the theory of colour and light, then he applied his knowledge to his painting. Seurat painted very small dots or dashes of bright colour, one on top of the other. Each small area of colour showed clearly next to the others. The painter thought that the viewer's eye would mix the colour. He believed that colour that is seen in this way is clearer and purer than paint which is mixed on a palette. Seurat's technique is obvious in this shimmering picture of the River Seine.

Shimmering pictures

Seurat often painted from the same place, in a park by the river. In this picture it is the freshness of a bright spring morning which has interested him. Colours glitter in the clear light. The water glistens with a million tiny reflections. Seurat has used dashes rather than dots in this painting, and he has used them differently for each part of the picture. On the water they are arranged horizontally, on the tree bark they are vertical, and in the tree tops the directions are varied. The dashes are evenly spaced all over the picture. Even the sail is dashed in, in shades of white. The dashes in the sky, in palest blues and lilacs, almost merge. The water, mostly greeny blues, has little touches of orange and red which flash and gleam. For the shadowed tree trunk Seurat has chosen reds and purples. The border is also in darker tones enlivened with flashes of red.

A Perfectionist

Seurat was a perfectionist in every way. He painted the darker borders around his pictures so that if shadows were cast by a frame they would not be noticed and could not spoil the picture. Sometimes Seurat painted the frame in dots as well! Seurat was a very quiet man. Few people knew him well, but many admired his work and were sad when he died suddenly, probably of meningitis. His ten-year career had been full of inventions and experiment.

Musées Royaux des Beaux-Arts de Belgique, Brussels

Spring Hoeing

Watercolour
Li Feng-lan

BORN:
1935

NATIONALITY:
Chinese

In China the majority of the people live in the countryside and work on the land.They work together, sharing the food they produce and also sending food to feed the people who live in the cities. Everyone must do their share of the work. Country workers — the peasants — are encouraged to be proud of their work for the community.

An opportunity to learn

In the part of China called Shensi Province, a community centre was built. For the first time, people had the opportunity to see paintings and to learn to paint themselves. One woman who tried painting was Li Feng-lan. She was born into a very poor peasant family before the revolution in 1949 in China. She did not learn to read until she was ten years old, but she was always making things, such as cut paper pictures to decorate the windows of her home. Then, in 1958, she joined an art class in her free time, and she learned to paint. She has painted hundreds of pictures since then.

Li Feng-lan always paints the countryside and the farm work that she knows well. She used to take her sketch book out into the fields, and make sketches in breaks from her work. She painted the pictures at night, when she had finished the farmwork and the housework.

A misty spring morning

The painting shows a team of women working in a field where a young crop is growing. A light mist swirls around the workers. Swallows dart in and out of the mist. Behind the figures the plum trees are in blossom.

Li Feng-lan has painted the scene in a very decorative way. The young crop spreads like a green sea all over the painting. The patchy mist reveals a broad curve of field, horizontally striped by the growing crop, curling away into the distance. The line of workers follows the curve. Their hoes reach out along it in a repeated pattern. Their bright jackets, clustered together, bring warmth and strength to the picture.

Landscape with Distant River and Bay

Oil on canvas 94 x 124 cm
Joseph Mallord William Turner

By courtesy of the National Portrait Gallery, London

LIVED:
1775–1851

NATIONALITY:
British

TYPE OF WORK:
landscape paintings, drawings and engravings

Joseph Turner's talent was recognized early in his life. He became a student at the Royal Academy when he was 14 years old and exhibited his first watercolour at the Academy a year later. When he was still only 32 years old he became Professor of Perspective at the Academy.

Travelling with a notebook

In 1792 Turner began a series of journeys which he continued throughout his life. He travelled first in Britain and later in Europe, making sketches and visual 'notes' of the landscapes which interested him. Turner looked for the beautiful in nature. Sometimes he sold his drawings and sometimes he made paintings from them himself, at a later date.

Drama and atmosphere

Turner painted accurate 'views' at first. He explored the landscape through thousands of drawings in a lifetime's study. Early in the nineteenth century the style of his painting changed. He began to concentrate on the way that places and events made him feel. This painting is one of his last. Here he uses his brush freely to show a golden landscape, with a distant hazy coast. Sky and land are scarcely separated. Thin cloud reflects the land and covers a sky of an intense blue. Turner does not say in the title of this picture which time of year he has painted. Which season do you think it was?

If you compare this painting with Brueghel's *Harvesters* (p. 18) you will see how similar they are in colour and composition. Both pictures have golden foregrounds and hazy distances, and yet how dramatically different they are. Turner was painting nearly 300 years after Brueghel, but even in his own time Turner's painting was considered extraordinary, and he had many critics.

When Turner died in 1851, the French painter Monet (p. 40) was 15 years old. We know that Turner's paintings influenced the Impressionist painters, especially Monet himself. Turner, however, unlike the Impressionists, made colour and light the main subjects of his work.

Musée du Louvre, Paris

The Harvesters

Oil on wood 118.1 x 160.7 cm
Pieter Brueghel

LIVED:
about 1525–1569

NATIONALITY:
Flemish

TYPE OF WORK:
paintings, drawings, engravings

The details of Pieter Brueghel's early life are not known, but he was probably apprenticed to a painter who had studios in Brussels and Antwerp. Brueghel travelled to Italy in 1552 and 1553, visiting Naples and Rome. He died when he was about 44 years old, and fifty of his paintings survive today.

High summer

This painting was ordered by a wealthy banker to hang in his new house. It is part of a set of paintings which showed different times and seasons of the year. One of the paintings may never have been completed, or has since been lost, but five have survived. In all of them Brueghel paints the seasonal activity in a long landscape with a river meandering away, or the sea in the far distance.

In this painting the sun beats down upon the harvesters. Some of them huddle beneath a tree, hiding from the midday heat. The sun is so high that we cannot see it. It casts barely a shadow. Heat soaks through the picture. The wheat is golden from root to tip. It glows with the heat it has absorbed, radiating warmth like the sun itself. In contrast, the fields in the valley look green and cool, and the distant coastline is hidden in a haze. This is the height of summer.

A speedy worker

Brueghel worked quickly, using thin paint, often allowing the undercoat on the wooden panel to show through the oil paint. The undercoat was a brilliant white mixture of chalky pigment and glue, called gesso, which was applied in layers to the wood. Shining through the oil paint, it adds sparkle to the paintings.

These pictures are now very popular, but Brueghel's work has not always been so popular. For a long time he was thought of as a peasant painter of ugly scenes and ugly people. He did not follow the fashion of other painters of his time, who made everything they painted appear beautiful.

The Metropolitan Museum of Art, New York. Rogers Fund, 1919

The Palm

Oil on canvas 114.3 x 147 cm
Pierre Bonnard

LIVED:
1867–1947

NATIONALITY:
French

TYPE OF WORK:
printmaking, paintings, posters and stage designs, illustration

Self-portrait. Private Collection.

Pierre Bonnard trained in law, but he took lessons at art schools in Paris in his spare time, against the wishes of his family. When he sold the design for a poster he decided to give up law and concentrate on art. Bonnard quickly became successful and his work was always popular. He also designed for the stage and even for the puppet theatre. At first he was better known for his prints and posters than his paintings. The detailed and decorative style of his early design work can be seen in later paintings.

Painting what he saw

Bonnard's pictures were of the world he saw around him. Though he was interested in the abstract work of other artists, he did not explore their ideas. He painted gentle indoor scenes, often in pale colours with mottled surfaces reflecting broken light. Many of these pictures include his wife, Maria Boursin (known as Marthe).

Bonnard began to spend time in the south of France and in 1925, just before this picture was painted, he bought a house on the Mediterranean coast. He also liked the light on the Atlantic coast, but the south-east suited Marthe's health better.

This painting has all the colour of a summer evening in the south of France, when bright terracotta roof tiles contrast with lavender shadows. Bonnard has made a soft oval frame of a green palm frond, tipped with golden light. Within this frame the sun, still bright, catches the rooftops and the soft stone walls. Away across the valley the evening shadows fall. In the foreground, a woman, perhaps it is Marthe, stands in the shadow and offers an apple.

Marthe died in 1942 and Bonnard was extremely lonely. He lived for only a few years after her, but he continued to paint and some of his greatest pictures were painted in these lonely years. In the year he died his pictures were exhibited all over Europe and in America.

Jawlensky and Werefkin in a Meadow

Oil on paperboard 32.7 x 44.5 cm
Gabriele Münter

LIVED:
1877–1962

NATIONALITY:
German

TYPE OF WORK:
paintings

Gabriele Münter was born in Germany, and spent part of her childhood in America. She studied at the Phalanx School in Munich, where she met the painter Kandinsky (p. 26). His teaching gave her confidence and from him came the idea that paintings could show how you feel about what you see. Münter went with Kandinsky and others, including Alexei Jawlensky and Marianne Werefkin to stay in Murnau, a little town in the mountains. There she collected locally made paintings on sheets of glass. She and Kandinsky tried glass painting and it began to influence the way in which she worked.

Colour tells the story

In this picture of her friends resting in a meadow in the mountains we see the effect of the glass painting. Münter began to paint areas of very clear bright colour, paying little attention to detail or to making objects seem three-dimensional. She used a strong black line to separate the blocks of colour and to define the shapes. If you half close your eyes, or look at the painting from a short distance, you will see how the colour glows, like painted glass. It is not simply the brightness of the colours the artist used, but exactly where she placed each colour that makes the picture so bright. Try covering the pink handbag with a scrap of white paper to see if that single patch of colour makes a difference to the painting.

There is little in the drawing of this picture to tell us its story. Jawlensky's straw hat and Werefkin's white dress suggest that it is summertime, and they rest rather wearily on the grass. The meaning of the picture comes from the way in which the colours are used. The sky is dark and the flowers and the meadow grass are bright in contrast. The light seems very clear and bright. Is it the heavy heat before a storm which makes the friends so weary?

© Gabriele Münter — und Johannes Eichner — Stiftung. Städtische Galerie im Lenbachhaus, Munich

Autumn Leaves

Oil on canvas 104.1 x 73.6 cm
John Everett Millais

By W. Holman Hunt. By courtesy of the National Portrait Gallery, London

LIVED:
1829–1896

NATIONALITY:
British

TYPE OF WORK:
paintings and drawings, book illustrations

John Everett Millais was, at 11 years of age, the youngest student ever to attend the Royal Academy of Art in London. There he met the painters William Holman Hunt and Dante Gabriel Rossetti. The three formed a group which they called the Pre-Raphaelite Brotherhood. They painted directly from nature, paying attention to detail and using natural objects in their pictures. However, they also used these objects to represent, or symbolise, their ideas. Their work caused quite a stir, and was not popular at first, but Millais later achieved great popularity.

Autumn sadness

The idea for this autumn painting seems to have come to Millais from several places. He wanted to paint the mood of late autumn, and the feeling of change and decay which it can bring. He had in mind, he said, some lines from the Psalms, and also poems by Alfred Tennyson and William Allingham which described autumn as a sad time. While on a visit to Tennyson, Millais helped him to sweep up some dead leaves in his garden. Later, he described the smell of burning leaves as, 'the incense offered by departing summer to the sky'.

Millais's wife, Effie, wrote that he had trouble getting started with this picture. His first idea had been to paint Effie under a cedar tree, then in a brown velvet dress under an apple tree. Finally, he set the painting in their Scottish garden at sunset.

Millais chose Effie's sisters and two local girls to pose for him. The girls, who still have the beauty of childhood, pile dead leaves onto a smouldering fire. The youngest holds an apple, the symbol of the harvest and also of sin and decay. The girls are rosy-cheeked and healthy, but their expressions suggest that they have glimpsed Millais's 'autumn thoughts'. For a moment the future seems to hold only sadness.

Manchester City Art Galleries

Painting Number 199. 1914

Oil on canvas 162.6 x 122.7 cm

Wassily Kandinsky

Bildarchiv Preussischer Kulturbesitz, Berlin

LIVED:
1866–1944

NATIONALITY:
born Russia, German citizenship 1927, French citizenship 1939

TYPE OF WORK:
paintings

Wassily Kandinsky was the first painter to work in an entirely abstract way. He describes coming home at twilight one night. Against his studio wall he saw a wonderful painting which, he said, had 'an inner glow.' He could see only colours and shapes and could not make out what the picture was about. Suddenly he realised that it was one of his own paintings, lying on its side. From then on he tried to make paintings which were about nothing except shapes and lines and colours. He had invented abstract painting.

From law to art

Kandinsky was born in Russia. He trained as a lawyer and then became interested in anthropology. He studied a Finnish tribe, and later he said that his interest in colours and patterns began when he saw their decorated houses. In 1896 Kandinsky saw an exhibition of Monet's painting (p. 40). It made him give up law, although he was about to become a professor, and leave Russia to study art in Munich in Germany. In 1922 he became a professor of drawing at the Bauhaus School, which was to play an important part in the story of art and design in this century. In 1933, when the Bauhaus was closed down by Hitler, Kandinsky left Germany and spent the last years of his life in France.

Something deep inside

Kandinsky was a religious and an emotional man. His abstract work, he said, came from an 'inner necessity'. It was not the world outside him that made him want to paint, but something deep inside him. Colour fascinated him and he explored the way that colours affect our feelings. He began to think that painting was like music, which you could listen to without wondering what it meant. Kandinsky published his ideas about art, and his work has influenced painters all over the world. He also wrote poetry and plays. This painting was called *Autumn* for many years. Now the experts are doubtful about Kandinsky's intention. Do you think that he still had the real world at the back of his mind when he painted it?

The Wine Harvest (Autumn)

Oil on canvas 275 x 190 cm
Francisco José de Goya

Museo del Prado, Madrid

LIVED:
1746–1828

NATIONALITY:
Spanish

TYPE OF WORK:
paintings, etchings and lithographs, tapestry designs

Francisco de Goya was a Spanish painter from Aragon. He became a pupil of the court painter Bayeu in Madrid, and later married his sister. Bayeu helped Goya to find work with the royal tapestry factory where he made more than sixty tapestry designs. He also painted portraits and religious pictures, and gradually his fame grew until he, too, became a court favourite. When he was 49 years old Goya became the director of the painting academy of San Fernando and four years later took over from Bayeu as First Court Painter.

A design for a tapestry

This harvest scene was one of Goya's designs for a tapestry. It is one of a set of four, each showing a season of the year. In this autumnal scene, a peasant girl brings grapes to an aristocratic family, perhaps the owners of the land, who have come out to watch the harvest. Goya designed the picture to be elegant and graceful. He was not trying to describe the hard work of the harvest, but to celebrate it. He has built the figures into a pyramid shape, with a diagonal line (the mountain edge) running through it. Many artists used this shape to balance figures in a picture. The danger is that the pyramid may not work — it sometimes seems to squash the figures inside it. Goya makes the pyramid light and graceful. He uses delicate floating colours. The figures are linked by arms reaching across space.

A darker side of life

In 1792 an illness left Goya deaf. His silent life gave him a greater understanding of people's sufferings. He started to paint strange, menacing pictures about the horrors of life. Goya succeeded at many types of work, from colourful tapestry designs to terrible etchings of war. In his portrait painting he tried to show the character of the sitter truthfully. Goya became famous throughout Europe, and his work still influences artists today. Eventually Goya left Spain and spent his last few years quietly in France.

Museo del Prado, Madrid

The Gust of Wind

Oil on canvas 40 x 58 cm

Jean-Baptiste Camille Corot

LIVED:
1796–1875

NATIONALITY:
French

TYPE OF WORK:
paintings

Musée du Louvre, Paris

Camille Corot's main interest was in the natural world. Sometimes his pictures included figures, but more usually he chose to explore the landscape. First he worked from direct observation, then he took his paintings indoors, where he would improve on nature, adding to the picture if he felt he needed to. He worked in gentle colours, preferring to paint dull days and evening light. Corot tried to show what it would feel like if you could step into his pictures, as well as what it would look like.

Catching the mood

In this picture we see a squally day in autumn. The trees are losing their leaves, and the world has turned from summer's greens to autumn's browns. The gust of wind of the picture's title bends the trees and grasses. The peasant woman pulls her shawl around her and turns her back on the wind, as she struggles to keep her balance. It is not a good day to be out. The sky, covered in scudding cloud, tells us that this gust has taken nobody by surprise.

In some ways this is an unusual picture. Corot has used very few colours to paint it. Apart from the pale blue behind the clouds, almost everything has been painted in soft pinky browns and yellowy creams. Do these colours help to suggest the mood of the day or does the painting seem dull? The scale of the painting is also rather unusual. The sky is a huge area and the trees are very tall. In comparison, the woman and the houses are minute. Dried grasses and boulders and a dirt road complete the picture. It is not what is usually thought of as a beautiful scene. Why do you think Corot chose to paint it? How much do you think that he may have 'improved on' nature in this picture?

Corot was successful in his painting career and his landscapes were popular with both the critics and the general public. He was also a popular man, and was known for his kindness to painters who were less fortunate than himself.

Musée du Louvre, Paris

Four Trees

Oil on canvas 110.5 x 141 cm
Egon Schiele

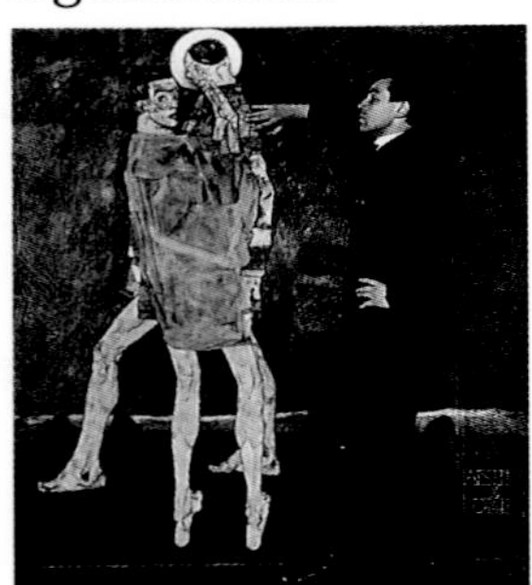

LIVED:
1890–1918

NATIONALITY:
Austrian

TYPE OF WORK:
paintings, drawings, poster designs

Bild-Archiv der Österreichischen Nationalbibliothek, Vienna

Egon Schiele died of influenza in an epidemic when he was only 28 years old, but he was already recognized as a very talented draughtsman. He was a very good, though not flattering, portrait painter. He was no kinder in the many portraits he drew of himself. He made hundreds of powerful drawings of both male and female nude figures.

When Schiele was 15 years old his father died. He missed him very much and never got over his death. He did not think his mother loved him. He did not think many people liked him and he seems not to have been an easy person to like. Schiele's drawing and painting style is hard and precise — it shows the way he felt about the world and the people he knew.

In 1915 Schiele fell in love and was married that summer. He was conscripted into the army, but despite the war he managed to continue to draw and his work sold successfully. His drawings at this time seem to show that he was happier, but they are no less powerful. Success and happiness did not last long. He and his wife died in 1918, within days of each other.

A draughtsman's landscape

Schiele's landscapes are as full of feeling as his figures. We can see his skill in drawing in this painting, called *Four Trees*. It is clear that the trees are chestnuts, the hand-shaped leaves which cling on, on this damp autumn day, are unmistakably chestnut leaves. The trees stand boldly against the sunset sky, each leaf and twig is clearly silhouetted. The sky and landscape are also 'drawn' in sweeping horizontal lines.

Schiele has chosen rich autumn colours — peaty brown, golden yellow and the rich russet red of the chestnut leaves. The design of the painting is simple. The sun, a bright circle, is placed just below the centre of the picture. The trees are symmetrically spaced on either side of it. The undulating lines of the landscape narrow towards the centre and focus our attention on the trees.

Österreichische Galerie, Vienna

A Man Stood in Front of his House with Rain Descending

Oil on canvas 243.8 x 152.4 cm

David Hockney

BORN:
1937

NATIONALITY:
British

TYPE OF WORK:
paintings, stage designs, etchings, photography

David Hockney has been a very successful painter ever since he left the Royal College of Art in 1962, the year in which he painted this picture. He won four major prizes in his last year at college and two years later he held his first solo exhibition.

Hockney was born in the county of Yorkshire in England. He says that wherever he lives he will always have his roots in Bradford, his home town. His large family was not wealthy, but he had a very happy childhood. The children were encouraged to join in the family arguments and Hockney grew up with strong feelings and opinions.

Watching the world

Hockney's ideas come from the real world, the people in it, the things they do and the places where they live. His ideas also come from other painters (he is a great admirer of Picasso), and from poetry. Hockney sorts out his ideas with the help of drawings and photographs before he paints.

In the pictures Hockney painted in his last year at college, he often used a drawing style usually found in comics or cartoons, like the simple, flat shapes you see here. He probably had in his mind the saying, 'An Englishman's home is his castle', when he drew the child-like cut-out castle with pointed windows. The man is dressed up as a 'joke' Englishman, wearing a traditional striped cricket blazer. He also wears late-1960's flared trousers and a funny little pork pie hat. He holds his tiny umbrella out in front of him. The rain is cascading down his face, indeed it has washed his face away! What is this all about? Perhaps the word IDIOT, printed neatly on his hat, is the clue. What sort of 'idiot' do you think he is?

In 1964 Hockney went to live in California, and his pictures were often of swimming pools and the bright colours of Californian sunshine. This picture was painted when English summers were what he knew best.

© David Hockney, 1962. Museum van Hedendaagse Kunst, Belgium

Landscape at Pentecost (Turamurra)

Oil on paperboard 83.7 x 111.8 cm
Grace Cossington Smith

LIVED:
1892–1984

NATIONALITY:
Australian

TYPE OF WORK:
paintings

Grace Cossington Smith was born in Sydney in 1892. She studied art in Sydney at a time when Australian painters were most interested in Impressionism. One of Cossington Smith's friends returned from a trip to Europe with copies of the work of Van Gogh, Gauguin and Cézanne. These painters were exploring the effects of colour and experimenting with ways of using paint to help them to express their feelings about the places they painted. Van Gogh often used very big swirling brush strokes. Gauguin used large, flat areas of colour. Cezanne saw the landscape like the surfaces on a cut jewel. Cossington Smith was interested in what these painters were trying to do. She visited Europe and studied in Britain and in Germany. When she returned to Sydney she began to work out her own approach to the Australian landscape.

A dry, dusty winter

In Europe and North America, Pentecost is a religious festival which falls in early summer. In Australia it takes place in mid-winter. Cossington Smith has painted a rolling landscape under a grey sky, but a little sunshine is getting through to light up the trees and the hillsides and to cast shadows in the dips. A long, straight road, cut deep into the red rock, leads to a homestead. Tracks along the road show how dusty it is even in winter.

Cossington Smith has used short brush strokes and thick paint to give some texture to the surfaces in her picture. Like Seurat (p.12), she uses the direction of the brush marks to help to describe the surfaces. She has used three broad bands of colour, the striking reds and yellows of the rocks, the blue-greens and blue-greys of the fields and hills, and the greys of the sky. The bands are broken into many patches, each a different shade. The changing colour describes the lumps and bumps, the hills and dells of this cool winter landscape.

Art Gallery of South Australia, Adelaide. South Australian Government Grant 1981

Ōi, from the Sixty-nine Stations on the Kisokaido

Woodcut print on paper 38 x 25.5 cm

Ando Tokitaro, called 'Hiroshige'

LIVED:
1797–1858

NATIONALITY:
Japanese

TYPE OF WORK:
prints from woodcut blocks

Ando Tokitaro was the son of an official in the city of Edo. His parents died when he was 13 years old, and he then chose to train as an artist. At the age of 15 years he was given his artist's name, 'Hiroshige' and his seal as an artist.He was competing with several other great Japanese printmakers and it was hard to become popular. Hiroshige admired the work of the poet Basho, who wrote short poems known as *haiku* about nature and his travels. Hiroshige began to make prints of landscapes and journeys and eventually his skills were recognized. This series of prints is about the long journey called Kisokaido. The series was begun by the artist Eisen, but Hiroshige completed 45 of the set of 69 prints.

A cold and lonely journey

The Kisokaido journey was particularly difficult, especially when winter set in. Here we see two travellers on horseback, led by two porters. The poor porters and the horses are ankle deep in snow. The travellers have tipped their hats over their faces to shield them from the snow which coats the whole world in a thick white blanket. The hats make the picture feel mysterious, as these faceless people trudge towards us.

Hiroshige has used the most delicate range of greys in this print. He has used stronger colours on the travellers and the pine cones, but the red seals against the grey and white make the scene feel even more wintry. For the Japanese printmaker, the seals were important. They were always carefully included in the picture.

Printmaking was a team effort. The artist drew the blocks and chose the colours. Other members of the team carved, coloured and printed the blocks. As many as ten blocks could be carved for each picture. The pictures had to be very carefully printed, one block on top of the other, so that each area of colour fitted exactly in place.

By courtesy of the Board of Trustees of the Victoria and Albert Museum, London

The Magpie

Oil on canvas 98.9 x 130 cm

Claude Monet

LIVED:
1840–1926

NATIONALITY:
French

TYPE OF WORK:
oil paintings, drawings

Musée du Louvre, Paris

Claude Monet is probably the painter most people think of first when the Impressionists are mentioned. The Impressionists were a group of artists who lived in and around Paris. They shared their ideas about painting, and often worked together.

A new vision

Monet tried to see the world with fresh eyes. He said that he wished that he had been born blind, and gained his sight when he was ready to start painting. In that way he would see things for the first time without knowing what they were. From the style of painting that he chose and developed throughout his long career, we can begin to see what Monet meant. He also said that he wanted to paint naturally,'...as a bird sings...'

Learning from nature

Monet may have wanted to paint naturally but he thought very carefully about every aspect of his work. He always painted from real life, often working out-of-doors, even in the coldest weather. One writer recalls seeing him with a foot-warmer, three coats and gloves, painting snow drifts! His life-long interest was in the effect that light had on the world he saw. He wrote 'I only know that I do what I think best to express what I experience in front of nature.'

This painting is all about light on snow. On a winter's evening, a setting sun turns the cloudy sky pale gold. The snow-clad ground, reflecting the sky, shimmers in gold and silver. Snow rests on winter trees, and drifts under the hedgerow. Monet has seen a cold, pale purple in the shadows. He has caught a magical moment in time with a few colours, which he has put on to the canvas with flickering strokes of the brush. The magpie, resting on the gate in the watery sunshine, adds to the feeling of 'the moment'. The bird will not stay when night falls.

Musée d'Orsay, Paris

Winter Landscape

Oil on wood 36 x 47 cm
Denÿs van Alsloot

LIVED:
1570–1627

NATIONALITY:
Flemish

TYPE OF WORK:
paintings

This picture was painted more than two hundred years before *The Magpie*. The painter, Denÿs van Alsloot, was one of several Flemish artists who began to paint simple landscape pictures of ordinary places, on ordinary days. It was this interest in the natural world which would lead eventually to Monet's vision of light and colour.

Van Alsloot's subject is similar to Monet's in *The Magpie*. There are trees and houses, and the sun is setting. The evening is cold. Snow and frost still cling to the branches, and icy water has flooded the fields. Someone has placed logs in the mud to make the footpath passable. This is a harsh winter.

A different way of seeing

If you compare the two paintings you will see how differently Van Alsloot and Monet saw their scenes. They were interested in quite different things. The most striking difference is the colour. *Winter Landscape* is hard and bright. It has been described as 'a frosted jewel'. *The Magpie* glows gently, almost dully in comparison. Which painting makes you feel colder? Which colours do you see on winter days?

The trees have been painted differently too. Monet has only suggested their shapes, but we know that every important trunk, branch and twig is there. In Van Alsloot's picture the lacy silhouettes of the trees against the sky are also important. Nothing is left to our imagination here. The artist has even painted the last few leaves clinging to the oaks. Broken stumps and gnarled roots balance the pattern of the treetops. Both artists have looked at a winter landscape, and seen beauty. Van Alsloot also saw that winter was a harsh and bitter enemy. Monet saw a world blurred and made gentle by a blanket of snow.

Van Alsloot was first known as a painter of religious scenes, especially of processions and fêtes. Later in his career he began to paint nature in a more realistic style, and he is now well known for his winter landscapes.

Musée du Louvre, Paris

Hoosick Falls in Winter

Oil on pressed wood board 50.2 x 60.3 cm

Anna Mary Robertson, known as 'Grandma Moses'

Grandma Moses at her Painting Table — © 1987 Grandma Moses Properties co., New York

LIVED:
1860 – 1961

NATIONALITY:
American

TYPE OF WORK:
needlework pictures, oil paintings, painting on tiles

Grandma Moses was probably the outstanding American 'primitive' painter in this century. She began to make pictures, teaching herself, in her seventies, and she continued until her death at 101 years of age. 'Primitive' painters work in a simple, often traditional, style. They are not usually formally trained.

Anna Mary Robertson married a farmer when she was 27 years old and raised five children. It was when she became a widow that Anna, now Moses, began to embroider pictures as a hobby. When arthritis made embroidery difficult, she turned to painting. Her pictures were about everyday events in the New England countryside, where she lived for most of her life. Her work was spotted by an art collector, who lent three of her paintings to an exhibition at the Museum of Modern Art in New York. Her pictures eventually became popular and well known to millions of people in Europe, as well as in America, on Christmas cards and calendars.

A simple style, a clear vision

The pictures were popular because they reminded people of the gentle life-style of bygone days. But it was "Grandma Moses's" (as she became known) ability to paint scenes in a clear, fresh and uncomplicated way which caught people's attention and imagination.

This picture of Hoosick Falls, covered in winter snow, looks very simple at first glance. The train, the wooden houses and the townspeople look childish and toy-like. However, Grandma Moses knew how to give her pictures space and feeling. The curving line of the river, the sweeping hills biting into the valley, and the clear, pale colours fading away to the distance, are cleverly planned. Little details tell the story — snow is caught on cabbages in the gardens, and the streets are slushy. Frozen grass stands stiff and still. The skeleton trees complete the chilly scene.

Grandma Moses worked from her memories and she also found ideas in newspaper and magazine stories and pictures. She painted 'to keep busy' and she produced more than 1500 pictures.

Musée du Louvre, Paris

Hoosick Falls in Winter

Oil on pressed wood board 50.2 x 60.3 cm

Anna Mary Robertson, known as 'Grandma Moses'

Grandma Moses at her Painting Table — © 1987 Grandma Moses Properties co., New York

LIVED:
1860 – 1961

NATIONALITY:
American

TYPE OF WORK:
needlework pictures, oil paintings, painting on tiles

Grandma Moses was probably the outstanding American 'primitive' painter in this century. She began to make pictures, teaching herself, in her seventies, and she continued until her death at 101 years of age. 'Primitive' painters work in a simple, often traditional, style. They are not usually formally trained.

Anna Mary Robertson married a farmer when she was 27 years old and raised five children. It was when she became a widow that Anna, now Moses, began to embroider pictures as a hobby. When arthritis made embroidery difficult, she turned to painting. Her pictures were about everyday events in the New England countryside, where she lived for most of her life. Her work was spotted by an art collector, who lent three of her paintings to an exhibition at the Museum of Modern Art in New York. Her pictures eventually became popular and well known to millions of people in Europe, as well as in America, on Christmas cards and calendars.

A simple style, a clear vision

The pictures were popular because they reminded people of the gentle life-style of bygone days. But it was "Grandma Moses's" (as she became known) ability to paint scenes in a clear, fresh and uncomplicated way which caught people's attention and imagination.

This picture of Hoosick Falls, covered in winter snow, looks very simple at first glance. The train, the wooden houses and the townspeople look childish and toy-like. However, Grandma Moses knew how to give her pictures space and feeling. The curving line of the river, the sweeping hills biting into the valley, and the clear, pale colours fading away to the distance, are cleverly planned. Little details tell the story — snow is caught on cabbages in the gardens, and the streets are slushy. Frozen grass stands stiff and still. The skeleton trees complete the chilly scene.

Grandma Moses worked from her memories and she also found ideas in newspaper and magazine stories and pictures. She painted 'to keep busy' and she produced more than 1500 pictures.

MOSES.